Atlantic Flyway

Atlantic Flyway

POEMS BY
BRENDAN GALVIN

Athens
The University of Georgia Press

Copyright © 1980 by the University of Georgia Press
Athens 30602

All rights reserved

Set in 10 on 12 point Monticello type
Printed in the United States of America

Library of Congress Cataloging in Publication Data

Galvin, Brendan.
   Atlantic flyway.
   (Contemporary poetry series)
   I. Title.
PS3557.A44A94   811'.5'4   79–3051
ISBN 0–8203–0501–4
ISBN 0–8203–0503–0 pbk

For My Mother and Father

Acknowledgments

Acknowledgment is given to the following publications in which poems from this book first appeared.

Ascent: "Shoveling Out"
California Quarterly: "Himself"
Canto: "The First Night of Fall," "An Instance," "Envy"
Chariton Review: "Triptych for Snowlight"
Chowder Review: "The Birds," "Hometown," "Homage to Henry Beston," "Little Solstice"
Crazyhorse: "Place Keepers," "The Others," "An Old Map of Fresh Brook Village"
The Georgia Review: "The Old Trip by Dream Train," "An Old Map of Barnstable County," "Insomniad"
Minnesota Review: "Fear of Firewood"
New England Review: "Fear of the Waldorf Cafeteria," "For a Little Girl of Pompeii," "The High School," "1847"
The New Yorker: "Young Owls" and "Woodsmoke"
Poetry: "Tautog," "Stethoscope"
Poetry Northwest: "Trying to Flatter Twelve Mile River"
Quarterly West: "Great Horned Owls," "Though," "The Migrants," "Netsilik," "Defending the Provinces," "Bear's Spring, the Way It Comes"
The Runner: "May Fog, Hill Training, the Orchard in Flower"

The epigraph to "1847" is adapted from Cecil Woodham-Smith's *The Great Hunger*, and I am indebted to that book and to Terry Coleman's *Going to America* for some of the historical information in Part 3 of this collection.

Contents

One

Great Horned Owls 3
Woodsmoke 6
An Old Map of Fresh Brook Village 7
Tautog 9
The First Night of Fall 12
Trying to Flatter Twelve Mile River 14
Little Solstice 16
Edge 18
May Fog, Hill Training, the Orchard in Flower 20
Defending the Provinces 21

Two

Stethoscope 27
Fear of the Waldorf Cafeteria 29
Though 31
For a Little Girl of Pompeii 33
The Others 35
Old Old Woman, Little Girl 37
Shoveling Out 39
Hometown 41

Three

1847
   1: *A Man from Adare, County Limerick* 45
   2: *Report of the Board of Potato Commissioners* 47
   3: *Steerage* 48

Himself   50
Insomniad   52
The Old Trip by Dream Train   54

Four

Netsilik   59
Bear's Spring, the Way It Comes   61
Envy   62
The High School   63

Five

The Migrants   67
Place Keepers   69
Pitch Pines   71
The Birds   73
A Triptych for Snowlight   75
An Instance   77
Homage to Henry Beston   79
Old Map of Barnstable County   82
Fear of Firewood   84
Young Owls   85

During southerly migrations up to 12 million birds leave Cape Cod per night.
Scientific American

In a world older and more complete than ours they move finished and complete, gifted with extensions of the senses we have lost or never attained, living by voices we shall never hear. They are not brethren, they are not underlings; they are other nations, caught with ourselves in the net of life and time, fellow prisoners of the splendor and travail of the earth.
Henry Beston, *The Outermost House*

If a blackpoll warbler were burning gasoline instead of body fat, it could boast of getting 720,000 miles to the gallon.
Scientific American

One

Great Horned Owls

1

A log shifting in the grate,
or some onyx-eyed gnawer
dropping around for suet,
I snap to under goosedown,
my breath stilled
in the near frost of the room.

A few hours ago,
the last streaks of February
stacked in the cut between hills,
and our small marsh tilted and took in
the reedy blatting of geese,

and now, maybe down off
Cathedral Hill, an owl
begins her midnight blue vibrato,
like a sound before sounds,
a five-part respiration of the earth.

2

What consolation is it
that they mate for life,
the male bowing and scraping to her,
renewing his vows
in the bottom nights of each year?

His courting gifts
are the whimper borne through the air,

the rabbit's imprint stopped
part way across snow,
and the bone spree slung as though
from a diviner's hand.

3

In March,
motherly, she'll ride
the jumble of sticks and pelts
she bumped a hawk for,
warming her egg
though she's sodden as a stump.

Winds crossing April will flirt
in tail feathers harmless as a hen's,
until one afternoon she walks off,
pumping her five-foot span,
and begins doting on
the owlet that hisses her home
to pin it in crossed wings

and pass it the brains of
that flicker who strops his beak
on our tin chimney these dawns,

and the warbler whose song
will be amputated mid-run,
and the unlucky leaf-treader

whose squeal of outraged dignity
will flare like a stain
through sleep,

because, just now,
from across the marsh,
the male floated back that same
pentamorous call,
dactyl, trochee,
a tremolo stitching the small hours together.

Woodsmoke

It drifts out like
the essence of a tree—
a spirit tree is
forking and branching
across these fields,

and I pull over on
this moment of lemon
dusk and new snow
reducing the town
to a huddle of cakes,

and listen for the solitary
plock of an axe
beyond the wind-rattled
hearts of weeds.

A tree drifts out,
slower than water locked
in this brook,
rooted in flames
as I am rooted in flames.

An Old Map of Fresh Brook Village

Sometimes, on a two-kingfisher,
double-your-luck day, I think
I can leap clear of concepts
and land on both feet
in a time when ponds on maps
looked like thumbprints,
and a triangle meant: hill.

The village is back there
somewhere, less than a crow's mile
from the checkerboard symbol for salt works.

If I can get there before
the railroad spreads in like dendrites
and the houses are flaked
for hencoops
or floated down the bay for
ships' chandleries,
and the burial vaults
are de-bricked for chimneys,

if my manners don't scare
some mooncusser's wife
into fisting a sockful of stones,

I can sit among apples or lilacs,
smoking with men
who can never quite shake
the mackerel scales off their sleeves;

I can love a grammar school of faces
open and honest as a woodcock's
for what they don't know
about things like internal combustion,

while rafts of oldsquaw and eider
rock on the bay
and wood pigeons cloud
the sun of the young republic.

Tautog

Capone-face, fish,
flabbergasted at being dumped
miles from the #3
can buoy
in half a beer case,
your mouth still chomping
as though on the memory of
corona coronas,
you bring back every muddy
high school punt
that squirted through my arms.

When you quit
this apoplectic puffing
it's going to be one on one
again, me trying to peel
your football hide with pliers
and slash the mastic from
fillets that bake
to a mouthful of petals.

Later, your life played out
into mine, in the dark
if a man comes to slap me up
mid-air, I'll know why,
my heels doing a dead beat
against this kitchen door
while he threatens
to up the vigorish and improve
my knees with a Louisville Slugger,

or if something hauls you
out of the mulch, a tail
joined to gills
by bones like a drawn-out
musical stave, you will
gloss its coat to a puddle
skimmed by rainy sky.

But no dream of
punishment or beauty
returns you to the stone bottom
and puts a sea clam back
in the pressuring clamp
of your mouth.

In a bucket of week-old rain
I found a grasshopper
clinging to a brown pine needle,
alive, antennae looped around
a water bead or tear,
but thought how senses leave,
bobwhite startling like
a detonated bush, how something
in me always wants to hire out
late and cheap as eulogist, or scrub
the lichen off stone lambs
and set a fallen marker
on its feet, dusting it off,
an arm around the shoulder—
as if it was a kid

thrown by a new two-wheeler,
and it could hear me
tell him, Try again.

The First Night of Fall

Each July, an evening arrives
with a warbler noodling a song
that resembles its flight over water,
and a cricket testing its flywheel.

Sun flares
in an outlying pool of the marsh
like a fire in a bucket.
A mosquito draws up to your ear
with a singular buzz on,
rubbing its limbs over
the same old story.

A small event at a time,
sleep comes to the weedy pond
at the top of your mind.
A bluegill's surface plip
widens,
a whitening loop
that fails to reach shore.

Before the spray of stars appears,
a heron that trailed its feet
all day in the face of a cumulus
limps down the skyline home,
and folds into its cloak.

In this illusory light
you are young again,
and your grandfather

has come back to watch over you
and hear in a crow's wings
the wrinkling of bombazine
an exciting woman wore.
He knocks his pipe on a stump,
that woodpecker
tapping back in the trees somewhere . . .

Later a small wind
wanders the house, shutting doors, sweeping
the blueprints for that day's disasters.

Trying to Flatter Twelve Mile River

Later you will touch on everything,
your surface
chameleon with sky-change
wrecking and building its
chance designs, all night
shooting gaps without
hesitation, haphazard
with end runs and hip fakes
only water has.

But how does one
compliment the universal
solvent pooling humbly
here among skunk cabbage,
lavish to backrowers,
oscillators, hoarding
depths and tunes,
waiting to leap and splash
into Cowfield Dazzler,
Gypsy of Ditches, and
First Rouser of Silt?

Belly-bumping at light's
pace, dragging glossy
overtones, so unlike us
you can never spread
yourself too thin or go
too far, you are sipped at
by rhizomes, entered by
splayfoot and muzzle,

while all that passes
through us are
deeply wading fears
and an occasional arrow of joy.

You give yourself away
as only a saint could,
and are elsewhere when
the first warmed-over
ephemerid wavers up
in a sizzle of wings,
each of your trickles
a filament in your brown
peroration,

while up near stars
there's a drop, then a
drop, in the cup of
an old leaf, till it tilts
away from that cold edge,
then a wriggle, a
salamander tremble
breaking into whatever
ways there are.

Little Solstice

The edge of the frost
grows up to windows
one thorn at a time:

albino corals, lace sharp as spurs,
the graveyard
of superstructure beyond:

woods like old roller coasters
and wrong cat's cradles
the cold preserves.

When the brass of
that other solstice
tames to a finch's twitter,

and every green is gone
but the olive black of pines against snow,

we fall in love with little ecstasies
that deny the day's pallor:

red lichen kissing logs
in a marsh fermenting reeds
and black water,

and the duff under scrub recomposing,
coming forward a piece at a time,

each double handful
resolving itself to a quail
with a trout-brown back,

the sentries stump-hopping,
transmitting the covey from one
cloud of brush to another,

and the bay
all morning concocting itself a tone
somewhere between the blue
of a jay's throat

and that fleeting indigo
on the shoulders of mourning doves.

Edge

Seventh sense
crawling my nape,
I turned and

heron, great blue,
apparition blue,

wizard head,
cautious strut

on the last edge of
open water,

my breath on tiptoe
through pale reeds.

Shank end of December,
I will take anything—

thread of tinsel woven
in a fled nest,

or nuthatch, the picky
crank,

but heron, blue as
the afternoon's lunar
fragment,

breast
deeply keeled for

long sails on the banked
nameless pastels of
evening!

To store in a ventricle
of memory,
here on this bend of water

wind will lick
to a playground for
skates and a shuttling puck.

May Fog, Hill Training, the Orchard in Flower

Each row of saplings
seems to arrive
like a white asterisk of surprise
beamed across distance,
and no bee box is heavy enough
to keep these hills from drifting off.

So, what looked like a loose,
thick bolt of velvet
carried over the shoulders
of two men
is an Aberdeen Angus bull
pondering mist.

Now you will have to sprint
from these high, bird-crossed acres
where the old ones have weathered
such hungers of mice and snow
they have learned an illusion of presence,
and seem to turn with you
for as long as you pass.

Defending the Provinces

The man on the city corner,
a shopping bag in each fist,
turns through all the compass points
until he falls;

on Main St. I can only walk north or south,
and when I drop, they know my name
and drive me home.

Give me Breughel the Elder, not Pollock
or a Santa Claus so drunk his breath could
take the paint off the crosstown bus.

You have to know whose labrador
is sprinting your fender neck and neck,

why Ellwood Gray claims he owns
Little Spectacle Pond.
                        You have to know
what a Chrysler marine engine
is doing in the Widow Wood's front yard,

and who burned all his laths to keep warm,
so had to pull the house down.

Let the village idiot sort the mail
and pass out jelly beans in church;

let the mash notes of Arthur Fisher
arrive at the homes of beautiful

high school seniors, complete with illustrations,
in plain brown wrappers,

                        and "the Mole Family"
and "Force-of-Gravity" live up to their nicknames.

Since there are no longer party lines,
the price of CB scanners must be drastically reduced.

And bring on the great weather: friends shaking out
the good word *inundated* between them
like a blanket out of mothballs.

                                When the Gulfstream
takes to the air, a flying green fetor
of ripped-out bayous trailing roots, we'll have
skies the color of Boy Scout troops
and skiffs slamming like loose bulkhead doors;

sand will walk the shore roads like men atomized,
wind will tune wires to the pitch of stress,
splitting TV faces at their laminated seams

while empty channels flood with remote news
and we wait for a streetlight to snap at the stalk
and send the picture diving into the tube.

Next day, since it makes a good story, we will say
we saw minnows swimming in roadside puddles.

I will write to our President if you will,
asking him to move everyone out of the Big Apple
and plant it with kudzu.

                         Sell the bridges for scrap
and let the rats clean up so in 200 years
guided tours can visit our national ruin,
our own Macchu Picchu,

                         and Americans, coming home
to their little towns, will tell how
last night on the highway, one star
over the bay seemed to move closer.

Two

Stethoscope

No one is home but this man
and his dogs, their mildly
reasonable eyes
lifting each time he moves,
two true believers
ready to follow, so benign
his mind returning
panics like a babe
waking in the Peaceable Kingdom.

Too peaceable. Hoping to divine
the inner necessities of
a few things, he puts on
his daughter's small, real
stethoscope, and after
the after-you routine
of man and dogs in a doorway,
goes dowsing for sound.
How, at heart, does the
frigidaire feel about
being a stolid but generous
belly; what can be said
in favor of the cold?

It is tuning its inner ear
to mile on mile of wheels
clicking down tracks;
but is that a dog
barking among trees between
the panels of this door,

or only the packed grains
dreaming a forest?
How much of this is
his own mallet and tympanum?
If he pries the panel
will evergreen flounce
into the room, and by what
act of will does he hold
his house together, and against
what, that the young dog
who barks at odd noises,
and the older, whose breed is
famous for saving children,
can't defend him?

Fear of the Waldorf Cafeteria

I am afraid if I go there again
and sit and stir my coffee
Les will still come in with his
1914 belted Fokker leather overcoat
and Shakespeare haircut,
and sit alone reading the *Sonnets
from the Portuguese*, the eyes above
his vague vandyke saying
there's no one home, he's gone
to stony lonesome, riding high,
everything he sketches
turning to cartoons, Hallmark
in his cards instead of Paris.
I am afraid that kid from
Mission Hill who hates himself
for broken teeth and the blue
tinge of his skin will
still come in, his brain
a steel machine flooding with
ignorant oil, and start on Les
again, and the counterman
won't stop crying
Toast the English! and the cop
out back, studded like a blue
vault door, will keep on
scoffing home fries, and I
will count the cars outside on
Huntington or dive into
Help Wanted though it's too late in
the day to look for work. Is that

the same couple in the corner,
black Museum School portfolios,
same rubber sandals, self-conscious
but loud about form following
function or the other way around,
and when do I
forgive myself my youth?

Though

Though pale light wanders
this water, and water wanders
among the burls of sand,
and the sun is
an old beekeeper
asleep on a stone wall,

though the breeze off this
eelgrass is like
the first kiss I thought
would last forever,

I think of what will come
to wither your face
and stumble my pulse
among its syllables.

Though your hand on my lips
stops my cursing
every brick by name
to bring it down,
and furls the red flag
of my fear,

we will be smoke
instead of understated
words for desperation and
desire,

      though I lift
my hands to the level of air
where your face might
suddenly appear,

                you
who divide the dark from
the dark awhile.

For a Little Girl of Pompeii

The dog's still jerking on his chain
because the slaves knew life comes
before duty. They are still running
from the sleepy forenoon
you've slept away for nineteen centuries.

Your rib cage got to me,
and your hands gathered before you
in a prayer to falling ash
or in the simple lifting of your tunic
to your face: a little girl asleep on her side.

It looks like there's a flower   .
growing nearby, but I'm not going to pluck
that consolation for you. Instead,
I'm going to make believe
you're real as this bad photo
makes you seem, not just technician's plaster
blown into the hollow where you were.

Real as graffiti on those walls, "Samius
to Cornelius, go hang yourself,"
real as the umbrella
Vesuvius opened above your head.

It's been worse. Pits
have been uncovered where you're multiplied
millions of times, not just in dreams,
not just by acts of random providence.

You're realer there than patios
the Prince d'Elbeuf
lifted from your marble town
because you're utterly without protection.

It's your ribs that get me,
moreso your hands in their small gesture.
I have one hand for my daughter, crossing streets,
but sometimes, from now on,
I'm going to make believe my other hand's
for you. To give me balance.
Between the two of you, you two could lift me.

The Others

This one was familiar,
and wandered the roads for
thirty years, January or June
regular as some Prussian
clocksmith's monster, a mute
in a hide getup

collected from tannery dumps
and pulled together
with thongs. He remembered
which side door
to pound for stew or
a gill of brandy, and would
wait under a tree,
nameless and harmless.

Hair matted, not quite
bearded, his hands chapped
and cracked like old potatoes,
he seemed older than any place
they might have kept him
for his own good,

and was found, finally,
by beagles running a break in
late snow, tobacco frozen,
jackknife a fistful of rust,
an inner pocket of bread heels
and leather scraps.

When I try to confront
my inner rabble, those sleepers
in the coalbins and barns
of childhood, vaguely guilty,
if only of being a side of us
to pin outmoded rags on,

he is always the one—eyes
full of the height
of twilit road ahead—who elbows
his way forward, their spokesman.

Old Old Woman, Little Girl

One is beginning to learn
what the other is forgetting,
one preparing to go
where the other has been,

and they feed each other
from twin kitchen chairs,
the space between
as clear as a sky beyond
two branches, one tapering out,
the second a nub
of everything possible,

while we stand
in the eighty years between,
thumped by abstractions,
in a crossfire of love and money.

Neither is always certain
who the other belongs to,
and with both it's a matter
of how many teeth, of when
to be put to bed,

of sharing the other's spoonful
like a secret withheld from us
because they are nearer
that point on the circle
where questions are useless,

where pleasure is
two voices rising and dropping
branch to branch
for the red berries of delight.

Shoveling Out

Before I picked bushels of beachplums
or delivered the news
to both sides of Hospital Hill
Sundays before dawn and six afternoons,
or shoved ranks of hanging lambs
that stuck to my palms like soap
and hacked up blue hubbard squash
thick as crocodiles,

money to my ears
meant the first hiss of snow
at the bedroom windows,
and toward dawn the plow bumbling
and scraping.

We had a route: kids raced
for the food inspector's house
because he paid off in coins
and quarts of milk, in doughnuts
that tore to incredible jellies.

I remember
flights of stairs and driveways,
but the names on those doorbells
are blank as this lawn,
forgotten as anything I ever saved for
when I dug myself at dusk
back up the stairs home
and unfolded the wet singles,
piling a dime on a dime over and over,

as though with the right combination
they would reproduce themselves
while the cocoa and kitchen range
fought my chilblains.

Now, still digging out,
no kids come
with socks on their hands,
dragging their fathers' coal shovels
deep as bushels.
Do they already know
whatever they stack change for
will expire, or get stashed
under the roof of
a widow's garage, as we knew then
not to race
for the cheapskate doctor's house?

Hometown

From the mayor who had himself roughed up
for votes, to George the fifty-year-old newsboy,
we lived with that town
like a man lives with a trick heart.

Of a summer morning, before you could make
your will on your grimy bedsheet,
liquid natural gas
might expand beyond anybody's needs.

When Ike came through his limousine didn't slow
to collect the bouquets;
brawls that erupted, ending when someone
turned yellow as the air,
were microcosms for the civic phobia,
though nobody put it exactly that way.

At least dread balanced out
against the boredom,
and kept us from tilting over in our places
in front of Peerless Drugs,
where the sidewalk
was seeping into our moonboots
and beginning the climb
to our Tony Curtis Cuts.

The Translux became a warehouse for hope chests
the same year a serious crowd
rolled in the aisles
behind the Rialto's new tabernacle doors.

From the cop on the corner
who hadn't cleaned his pistol in fourteen years,
to Donny Tish-Tosh with the sewn-up pockets,
everyone knew there were two ways out of town:

"Character," by Albert Norton Parlin,
was chiseled on the face of the junior high;
translating it correctly, you could sieze
the hot chicken Life
before it got dropped in someone else's pot.

Or, picking whiffs of fast money off a breeze,
you could cure driveways with motor oil
the first shower would reclaim,

like the gypsies nobody heckled
when their Chevies passed us heading anywhere,
a set of mooncat eyes in a rear window
dragging our tin hearts clunking up route one.

Three

1847

1: *A Man from Adare, County Limerick*

> Halfway down Constitution Hill the report of a pistol was heard. . . . Queen Victoria stood up, and said to the page accompanying her, "Renwick, what was that?" "Your Majesty has been shot at," replied Renwick.

It wasn't loaded, or else
loaded wrong, and the man
from Adare was mentally
deficient, maybe
from boiling nettles behind
a bush or begging from inside
a hollow tree while his family
flapped in rags across a field,
hopping barefoot, hunting
row to frozen row
for one glabrous turnip.

Maybe he'd just been skinned
by a passage broker in Liverpool,
and a crimp ran off with
his sea chest while mancatchers
on each arm were trying to pull him
two ways to innkeepers.

Shoveled out, improved off the land,
too poor to be ballast for
a Black Star packet, his fate in
the failed potato, maybe he survived
the season of blackberries
while his children stared
like storybook rabbits

from under a scalpeen: his own
walls thrown on a ditch by
crowbar brigades, the landlord's
payment for rent owed.

Sir Robert Peel has a smile
like the silver plate on a coffin.
Indian corn is his brimstone,
and pokes through a child's
belly like nails through a sack.
When he laughs it's time
to finish the raw cabbage
and start on the seaweed, it's time
for the Dearth and Scarcity Prayer,
for black leg and black fever,
jaundice and the bloody flux,
road fever and typhus.

If Your Majesty pressed her palm
to the hollow of this updrawn
shoulder blade. . . . Heaven tugs
on invisible wings while Hell
drags at the heels,
but there's no tear, only the stare
and muslin pallor, the senile
gape of the man from Limerick's
bald, bearded daughter.

2: *Report of the Board of Potato Commissioners*

If, because of static electricity
generated by locomotive effluents,
or the mortiferous vapours of
blind volcanoes beneath the earth,
or from the guano of sea fowl
or the potato dropsy or other causes,
your crop is diseased, avail yourself
of a rasp, one square of linen cloth,
one hair sieve or cloth strainer,
two tubs of water and a griddle.
Now grate the unspoiled crop finely
into a tub, wash, strain,
again wash and strain, then dry
resulting pulp on griddle over
slack fire. Milky starch
precipitated in wash water, when
mixed with the dried pulp
of peas-meal, oatmeal, or flour,
makes wholesome bread or
farinaceous spoon meat. Sliced
potatoes soaked in bog water or
oven dried, or spread with lime
and salt, or treated with a mixture
of vitriol, MnO_2, and salt—
said mixture producing chlorine gas—
or baked 18-22 minutes on your cabin fire
at 180° F. . . . All true Irishmen,
we are confident, will exert themselves
to all we recommend, though

there may be a deal of trial and error
at first. If you don't understand
these directions, consult your priest
or landlord.

3: *Steerage*

If you could set stones on the Atlantic
from Liverpool to Grosse Isle
or New York, some would have graves.

In steerage the luckiest girl
got wedged between her brothers,
and lived despite Holloway's Pills
reputed to cure twenty-three things
worse than the Earl of Aldborough's liver.

Born unlucky, some slipped overboard
weighted with shot and unshriven,
taken by ship's fever
or water bunged in old sperm oil casks.

An orphan could get a customized name
in New York, and One-eyed Daley's
ticket for Detroit could end him
in Albany forever.

Grosse Isle seems to float
its white chapel and fever sheds
on a green shimmer in the St. Lawrence.

Everywhere you step
into the indentations under grass.

Himself

I light up a hooked, bunched thing
he brought from Ireland, its bowl in my hand
like an old laborer's knuckle
in the clutch of a child.
He would point this pipe stem
at my jiggling foot and say,
"It's the St. Vitus' Dance."

When my shoe feels the air out
for a rhythm it can't quite capture,
I hunt up the photo of Greenhorns
that emptied me the first time
I looked into faces of steerage.

But he is the never-there,
an absence even in these snapshots
yellowed as though in some
nicotine fit of time.
His wife twists her arms together
until they are white as parsnips,
and stares to her left as if
he might suddenly appear,
or as if, in the black box's eye,
she can see the buried childhood of their sons.

Carved briar warm in my hand, a blue tobacco tin
turned up in a back room,
but no face, no habit good or bad,
a grown-over legend like his bog-fed garden

where skunks lick turtle eggs
dry as his grandson's memory.

All his history, smoke from his barn's
spontaneous combustion and the black plume
off the Boston-P'town boat crossing the bay,
summer 1910, Himself
taken in by the air, and these hills
naked as his home county after the English axes.

This pipe, too, smoked in the Model A
his daughter wheedled him back to Boston in
at holidays, where he galloped me on
the black saddle of his brogan;
and when I drummed my feet at table,
where nobody spoke,
his was the voice in the black toe
that tapped my knee to say,
"Keep your feet at ease."

Insomniad

This late, things reduce to black and white:
stars casting their fires, the earth
an occluded mirror for the moon,
and the mind stumbling among
the consequences of a few square miles.

Now it's on Corn Hill Beach,
among packs of hudsonia where one October
I scared up a flock of early snow buntings.
It's pitying city crows, thinking how birds,
like people, can be luckier
in their choice of place than others.

Any second the mind might decide
to walk the back way to Duck Pond,
re-laying B & M tracks it'll have to cross,
then putting an ear to iron
for the far rumble of the Thursday freight.

When it stops to set a penny on that rail,
it slices thirty years off
this end of my life. The mind,
with its two-edged sword, can do that,
and recall my fear of derailment and prison,
something I read about French kids,
a Nazi train, and carpet tacks.

It never got to the pond. It never does.
Here it is outside the Square Deal Store
bankrupted before I was born.

Every night Bill Patrick put a lamp
in that window. Bootleggers read by it
which way to go. Later their product
convinced Bill to keep *how many* dogs
on one license? The mind wants to know.

It paints me into its corners
with the facts: my father's gone,
one old dog's "put to sleep."
It adds up cars and mortgages to prove
I've gotten this far by subtraction,

tells me my greatest fear is
that the kids aren't going to surpass me,
warns against trading my son's punches so hard.

And now it jerks me around, asking why I worry
when so many stars have died
to evolve these moments from their dust.

Not monogamous, it wants
to know if light from a girl's sweater
in one of these groves
twenty-five years ago
leapt from a constellation no one named.

The Old Trip by Dream Train

Engine and tender, old loaf-shaped Pullman.
I am making the trip alone
because of the house a dream within this dream
keeps erecting in my sleep.

It is always barely April, but at loading docks
behind the church-topped mills, in the cinders
and shattered weeds, it is late November.

No one is on the streets, no one's not working,
and the workday flashing past looks empty,
the storefronts blind. Not one pane of forty-eight
in a factory window winks; just row on row,
banked like the pigeonholes
in a postal clerk's nightmare.

In a side yard a hairless, vested man
rakes among shadows eloquent as the clang
of steel doors. There are joined angles of bridges,
tanks with coolie hats, a distant refinery
like stacked poker chips,

but always that house, white in April sunlight,
nearly perfect except for broken slats
in the green, nailed shutters.

Then the piney backs of towns, and blond fields
where rocks seem to crawl out of their shadows,
and the slow progressions into small, identical

cities of brown bungalows and triple-deckers,
clatter of Redcaps' dollies, arrival and departure

through which I see the shadow of a crow
crossing white shingles in light so clear
it could be bottled and sold.

Switchyards and sidings, men working gears
with levers, municipal power blocks, trestles,
at one stop the illusion of slipping back
when the cars alongside begin to move;

finally the coast, where a tug trundles upriver
and one seabird crosses high and slow,
a hint of prehistory in its flight,

then cranberry bogs, ditch-ruled and crossed
with levees supporting pump houses,
a set of iron wheels stunned in sunlight.

I try to see the roof of that white place,
the red brick chimney's shadow,
the rainstreak of mortar like a second shadow.

Under cirrus brushwork the creeks
crawl into harbors, their soft tides
feeling seaward in various blues, opening out
under sky opening out.

Crossings too small for gates and lanterns blur by,
each with its warning X,

and one by one, joined by railside wires,
minor stations appear on the line,

    a country of white houses whose one-story
    bedrooms and late ells meet their barns,
    whose oil drums sit on sawhorses.

I stop this trip by its pullcord, and step down
to a sooty cream station trimmed in maroon,
a coalbox alongside, and walk up a two-lane road
nothing is moving on.

The light is always April, chilled amber,
the air headier than I imagined.
Beyond the Big Dipper Dancehall, torn
to its baseposts thirty years ago,

I turn onto a sand road, pass cabins shut
till June, and Ed Mather's place;
he elected to live up hollow from everything
but a deer run and weather.

If I find that house where locust trees
shadow the flaking paint,
will I pry its green storm door and break
the frosted pane over the inside knob,

and enter rooms abandoned to mothballs and
mousedirt and that gray matter that springs out
on old shoes, and call that warehouse
of sheeted furniture home?

Four

Netsilik

Sea level, top of the world.
Beyond teeth of blue ice
thrown up and broken
where water faced off with land,
one dog. Then a man,
in a breathtaking wind.
Inside the wind,
souls already taken
unreel their endless necrology
to his ears.

In the lulls,
dots and dashes of snow
spit from a cloud mass
stacked above the world.
The sea groans through snow-ice.
The dog drops his nose,
inhales the blowhole: seal.

Under his sealskin
the man grasps a three-pronged,
hollow-centered star
of caribou bone.
He prods the dog away with
his spear's blunt end,
and plumbs the hole's angle
all the way to water
where sharp and blunt nose meet.
His breath whitens his upper lip.
He studies the slit-eyed distance.

Five hundred miles from the nearest tree,
he tamps the blowhole lightly with snow,
and reaching into himself,
spits in his palm,
freezing a snip of feather
to the bone tripod
he sets on the loose-packed snow,

and waits for the one breath
that might lift
swansdown from the star of bone.

Bear's Spring, the Way It Comes

Earlier than that bird he hears
but never catches snipping at the end of town
like scissors at newspaper,

prior to that cloud that passes over,
a bunch of finches in it
trying to re-invent sewing machines,

he's up and gone,
like someone who had to leave town
by a bathroom window.

You can see brown and seedy
around every tree
he tried to curl up under,

and how he prinked away,
expanding the tracks of skunk and dog,

those wisps of his blue snooze
still hanging three feet above ground—
he must have crashed somewhere:

listen hard downfield
beyond those fat ducks and their patter—
old men in the sun by the cigar store—

beyond those steaming mounds
or piles of underwear,
and you can hear him taking sips,

letting it all come in.

Envy

Night in the outskirts,
rut and dust, dead end.

Prickling weeds crowd
the dark green fence.

A house here once; now,
dry leaves hang

between the palings
someone kicked in.

Nobody comes. On the
splintery creosote pole

there's not even an old
barrel hoop backboard

to impede the climb
up spikes to the bulb

under the rippled tin
where the hot June bug

spins forever.

The High School

Like a halfback
who gives himself away
when he's going to carry,
there are girls behind that glass
whose eyes glaze
when they pass the best boys.

There are boys who will
walk in front of moving cars
because they're immortal
as vacationers,

and teachers reduced to gossiping
over the love-lives of
their charges: all
is as delicately arranged
as the molecular
structure of a bubble.

Outside, their mufflers
like prolonged smokers' coughs,
their tires edged onto grass,
the dropouts' morning.

Exempt from class, insiders
smoke at The Pit
and look out at the one
who peels his Harley
down the strip,
leaping it over bumps
installed to slow him.

Now he returns,
as at night many return
to break these bottles
in tributes equivalent
to votive candles.

A snub-nosed car
parked across the exit
is a way of asserting
existence and leaving the others
to get out as they can:
evidence that nobody
wants to go,
though everyone knows
the talent scouts
wait elsewhere.

Five

The Migrants

Aspersion growing all summer on the sidelines
of tennis courts,

odor of calumny heavy above the valleys,
finally, in a room saved by thermopane

from the vast pollination of evening light—
the man who had been to China

still going on about optional nudity—
he remembered the birds. On barrier beaches,

moors and wet marshes, everywhere that is pathless
and interrupted by water,

they would be coming on, the brief ones
named for a habit or voice, their beaks

like the tools of a forgotten craft,
their eyes lit with the moon's intensity.

Birthed from eggs like speckled stones
the north coasts have rounded,

they would whirl and lift as though
at the whisper of *Patagonia*,

their flight a wind-preened coherence
on the lengthening sky. They would come down

spraddle-winged and atilt
on bars whorled with the salt's thumbprint

and fog-furred tidal flanks,
berm pickers, wind-ups, scramblers and dippers,

the surf's one patrol, to sleep tight-bunched
as periwinkles before steering

down the longitudes.
Thinking of them, he thought how a man

can turn back to the world of men, as though
the blue book of fall had opened in his hands.

Place Keepers

Gray day, slow November hours.
The sea must be smoking
all the way out to the Banks.

Two cars in the beach lot.
In patched waders,
in water to her hips, the widow
who fishes with sand eels
she scratches up for herself,

and half a mile down the flats,
a man like a god
walking among a tranced flock, laying hands
upon each Canada goose without one
lifting off, the tide shrinking from him
beyond the final tumble of the jetty.

No miracle because, closer,
the birds are black-and-white effigies
staked in mud; at jetty-side,
in a stone blind under a stone-colored
blanket, his thermos and dog.

His breath is laced with rye.
His hat mimics fallen leaves; the loops
on his sand-colored vest are charged
for birds. Now he comes back for the jug,
his rosy Hello to the dog
visible in the hanging droplets.

The widow's beachfire
struggles through broken fish boxes.
She watches her pole
for the deep flex of winter flounder.

Pitch Pines

Some trees loft their heads
like symmetrical green bells,
but these, blown one-sided
by winds salted out of the northeast,
seem twisted from the germ.
Not one will lean the same way as another.

Knotted but soft, they mingle
ragged branches and rot to punkwood,
limbs flaking and dying
to ribs, to antlers and spidery twigs,
scaly plates slipping off the trunks.

Hanging on, oaks rattle maroon clusters
against winter. But these, resinous in flues,
blamed for a history of cellar holes,
snap in the cold and fall
to shapes like dragons asleep,

or thin out by dropping sour needles
on acid soil. For one week in May
they pollinate windows, a shower
that curdles water to golden scum.

From Bartholomew Gosnold's deck,
Brereton saw this cape timbered to its shores
with the hardwoods that fell to keels
and ribbing, to single meetinghouse beams
as long as eight men.

Stands of swamp cedar, cleared for cranberries,
were split to shakes or cut lengthwise
for foundations, while sheep cropped
elm and cherry sprouts
and plows broke the cleancut fields.

Fifty cords at a time, birch and maple
melted bog iron in pits; elm and beech
boiled the Atlantic to its salts; red oak
fired the glassworks at Sandwich—

till the desert floundered
out of the backlands and knocked
on the rear doors of towns
and this peninsula drifted
in brushfire haze,

and, clenching their cones
under crown fires, the grandfathers
of these pines held on until
heat popped their seeds
to the charred ground.

The Birds

Seeing them corner above fields,
black stars across the morning,
sometimes you'd gladly relinquish
weight of your self-possession
to hover three feet from anything
and be classified rare-to-occasional,

to desert glyph-printed snows one day,
a dot in a quick ellipsis across inlets,
your eyes alert
for heat wavering off savannahs.

Whatever their thoughts, they are never edged
with the scalloped green of money;
no bird violates another
with the inflections of small print;
singular or flocked,
they aren't compared with sheep.

Watching them, you see how their
third step in air
is hardest,
how it puts the boiled-egg face
on every day to flight.
Master it and it's goodbye to everyone
scrubbing at shadows.
You could live on nothing down
and pay only if caught,
you wouldn't be
a lentil in life's great stew anymore.

Think of freely backsliding, of countering
the food-gatherer's monotony
with the new indirection of your ways.
You could perform the herring gull's
high-stepping run,
his oyster drop on the uprise
and brief earth touch
to shake the essence from the broken shell.
You could be hang gliding
above ice piled in harbors like
white grand pianos,
or breasting thermals where sun
rousts vagrant ground fog.

You could be
the least tern who plucks
the edge of the sea's potlatch,
or the egret in its pool
like your spirit's sudden cry at sloughed confusion.

A Triptych for Snowlight

1

Are these the same chickadees who rolled
in the wet cabbages
and tracked down June bugs half their size?
Caught like them
between one wind and another
feeling us out
like products each means to buy,
there is just enough time
to relearn the chestnut streaks of
a fox sparrow and
the cardinal's Assyrian beard
before the sun dissolves
in albuminous snowlight.

2

Now caterpillars of snow
cling to every branch, intending to stay, and wind
begins sneering beneath
eaves and sills.

Is some pale wretch
floundering to her knees out there,
a small bundle of dreams
swaddled in her arms

as the woods tilt a new way
to the chonk and sizzle of ice in the flue,
heaven's crockery
thrown down on our heads?

3

Motes are jeering.
Pips who razz snow though it tries
to snuff them everywhere
are tugging the light,
even the shy redbird
is tucking light back into place.

On the still life of the mulch,
sun ignites citrus and apple skins,
and a crow puts on
the brow I wore all night
and walks the gangplank of a broken pine.

An Instance

Once only
I woke in wind
dashing the pines
and could just make out,
beyond pines and the wind,
a blue-white
constellation
navigating breathlessness,
some knarr or coracle,
a star boat
tracking that calm
in a current of its own,
beams studded with light,
sail tips and starred
mast glittering with cold.

And if
the Hunter's sword
isn't merely gas-glow,
if the beaten animal
aloft in his grip
is more than nine
inconspicuous stars,
then a woman cradled
that tiller in her arms,
her hair afloat on
the slipstream,
and a man at
the beast-headed prow
leaned for headlands

where most nights
the dark
is as evenly starred
as a geode's inner face.

Homage to Henry Beston

> The crashing tide not only claimed beach cottages, but also took with it part of Cape Cod's literary history, a small cottage in which 50 years ago Henry Beston wrote *The Outermost House*, a naturalist's view of a year on the great beach.   —news item

Hoping to shake a few hours
out of the intricacy
we live by,

I walked out to your "National Literary Monument"
last September,

wondering if you thought
Scolopacidae a cumbersome name
for the least sandpipers

risking gregarious fractions of an ounce
around my feet,
at the last instant lifting
with one will
to the group's synchrony.

I thought of how the *Pequod*
would have stunk,
how a shack is

a shack no matter who
screws a bronze plate to it,

how these are the places
where the thing gets done.

*

A wave rolled sea-raised dunes aside
to disinter and float
a ship's boat whole,

and you knew this geological one-acter
would close in some atrophying weather,
this first arm of America
dispersed in sediment.

But what arrivals in that going!
Seaward, on the blue heights of October,
that one-to-a-life flight of swans,

and the tundra's belling tribes
pouring down the rivers of the air.

Knowing both your rooms
would strew Nauset marsh

like drift the sea brought down
from Matinicus to your fireplace,

you weighed the reek of a corrupting gull
with the savour of wild pinks,

and read in de-creation
creation's pretext.

    *

I keep looking after
the young men and women going alone
into duneland, wondering

which backpack hides the notebook,
who recalls the last time
not even distant business
whined at the porch of the ear,

that one for whom some bird
the size of a baby's fist
may wring itself
for song
from the floating ridgepole of your place.

Old Map of Barnstable County

It doesn't show
how the cold edge of starlight
pierced woodpiles,

or the boy forking hay
who one afternoon cries out to no one
on the shore of Still Pond
and runs away to sea,

but crawls ashore years later,
to lie under this mapmaker's
pinpoint, which stands for "humane house,"
and gasp white-eyed on the straw floor,
his hands scrabbling his chest
for its breath.

Who would believe,
on this mapmaker's Atlantic
which looks safe as a strip of corduroy,
a schooner is floundering,

and soon heartbreak will walk
the sand roads up hollows
to Mrs. Small, Mrs. Snow, Mrs. Dyer,
sea widows whose lives will go on
in ways the cartographer's black squares
for houses can never explain?

A red dot for each vessel lost
would turn this map
to a rash like scarlet fever,

quick as a camera's shutter
that sea would close over islands,

and the griefs that went by the names
beside the black squares
would move on to other squares,

as on later maps
even the black squares
will have moved on.

Fear of Firewood

Because I have listened
to the trees' unceasing palaver,
and seen how their crowned stumps
in lapsed or returning light
appear to move closer to my house,
I put off splitting the dry cords until
one morning I look in a puddle
and see water stunned, ready to be
something I can hold in one hand.

While the bow saw exacts cries,
I watch for a trickle of blood.
A knot may cleave on a profile
remembered from some waiting room.
Working a trapped wedge free,
sometimes I'm afraid
the log will close on my hand
and never let go.

To warm me a little,
every day something dies.
The inner life of trees
cools and congeals in my flue,
and builds
on its harbored revenge.

Young Owls

Now crows mill blackly above them,
yawking as though
something is stuck in their craws,
and a panic of baby white
floats off the nest as if
struck in midflight.

But they are there,
trying deficient wings
and feet like goalies' mitts
at the nest's brink,
trying a gargle of little bones
and a stare like corpse candles,
their black pupils fixed in yellow.

They sit it out,
or lean into the future,
waiting for their buff feathers
to straggle downhill through scrub
till they are dressed like bark.

Visitations of neither
luck nor wisdom, they mean
no frogs in the garden this year,
no hunting the slope under the nest
for lady slippers
langorous with spring.

Dropping to berry tangles
on feet that later, quicker,

will snatch June bugs from the air
and flip them like popcorn
to their beaks,
they waddle toward dusk

and clutches of young terns
in the hollows on Egg Island,
fuzzy about how shadows
drop out of the sun,
how nothing in this world
gets out of its life alive.